psyched for science

Super Science Projects About Weather and Natural Forces

Lorraine Jones

the rosen publishing group's

rosen central

new york

To GBTG and to my aunt who taught me how to weather the storms of life.

Published in 2000 by The Rosen Publishing Group, Inc.
29 East 21st Street, New York, NY 10010

First Edition

Library of Congress Cataloging-in-Publication Data

Jones, Lorraine.
   Super science projects about weather and natural forces / Lorraine Jones.—1st ed.
      p. cm. —(Psyched for science)
   Includes bibliographical references and index.
   Summary: Introduces the basic concepts of meteorology through hands-on activities and research projects.
   ISBN 0-8239-3105-6
    1. Weather—Experiments—Juvenile literature. 2. Science projects—Juvenile literature.
   [1. Weather—Experiments. 2. Experiments. 3. Science projects.] I. Title. II. Series

   QC981.3.J65 2000
   551.5'078—dc21
                                                                99-043742

Manufactured in the United States of America

contents

introduction

Weather Is Everywhere

Weather is one of the most influential forces in nature. It determines how our plants grow, the

quality of the air we breathe, and the places we live. It influences and shapes a host of other things around us. Weather can affect us in a variety of ways, from rain canceling a picnic to tornadoes destroying our homes. Everyone has been affected by the weather—it is a "substance" of life.

In this book, you will study weather through a number of experiments and activities. This will not only involve direct observation and experimentation but will also require research, some of which you can do at your school library. However, for the best results, you will need access to the Internet, which contains vast resources for the study of weather.

A word of caution: You must be very careful when doing any experiment or activity. Whether you are dealing with chemicals indoors or observing weather outside, follow the safety precautions in this book and use common sense. Always wear protection for your eyes and body when performing experiments involving chemicals or water. Protective gear includes safety goggles, rubber gloves, long sleeves and pants, and hard shoes. When outside, take great care not to place yourself in danger of being caught in a thunderstorm or where lightning is likely to strike.

1 Create Your Own Weather Instruments

Weather forecasters base their predictions on readings from instruments designed to give them information about current conditions. Most weather forecasters use specially designed instruments, but you can predict the weather fairly successfully by making your own instruments.

In this activity, you will make a simple barometer (for measuring air pressure), thermometer (for measuring air temperature), wind sock (for measuring wind), and rain gauge (for measuring rainfall). You will use these instruments in Experiment # 2 to predict the weather.

What You Need

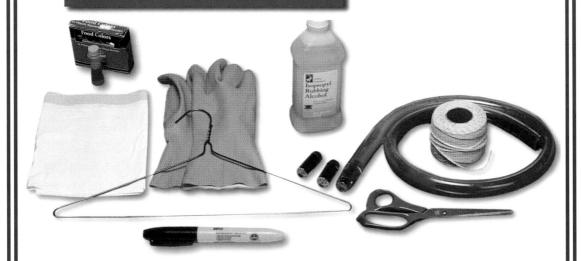

- A clear, flexible plastic tube, approximately 4 feet long and 1–2 inches in diameter (available at hardware stores)
- Three stoppers to fit the ends of the tube
- Water
- Scissors
- Rubbing alcohol
- Food coloring
- Heavy string or twine
- A heavy-duty trash bag or other light-weight plastic material such as Visquine (available at hardware stores)
- A wire hanger
- A clear plastic cup
- A jar or pitcher
- A waterproof marker

Barometer

#1 Cut the clear plastic tube to a length of 3 feet. (You will use the remaining 1 foot to make the thermometer.) Make sure to wear eye protection when cutting the tube, or ask an adult for help.

#2 Put some water in a jar or pitcher and add a few drops of food coloring.

#3 Bend the tube into a U shape. Pour the water into the tube until it is about half-filled on each side. Put a stopper in one end and make sure that it is sealed as tightly as possible.

Believe it or not, this is a barometer! The air pressure on the unstoppered side will make the water move up and down. That is the reason the stoppered end must be secured very tightly, or it will push out the other side when the air pressure changes.

#4 Tie the barometer to a tree, making sure that the tops of both ends of the tube are at the same height. Using a waterproof marker, mark fifty lines 1 millimeter apart up and down from the current height of the water to get a base value. This will tell you how much the air pressure has risen or fallen the next time you measure it.

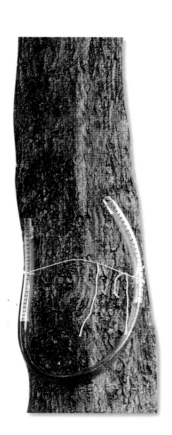

Thermometer

#1 Use the remaining 1 foot of tubing. Plug one end of the tube with a stopper. Make sure the stopper fits tightly. This will be the bottom of the thermometer. Pour enough rubbing alcohol into the tube to fill it halfway. Make sure to wear safety gloves and glasses, or ask an adult for help.

#2 Add a small amount of red food coloring and seal the open end of the tube tightly with a stopper.

#3 Tie the thermometer to a tree and attach a piece of paper behind it with lines drawn 1 millimeter apart. You will use this to determine the temperature.

#4   Call a local office of the National Weather Service or check the radio for the current temperature. Write this down on your thermometer chart and mark the current height of the alcohol in the tube. This marking represents the current temperature. Do this over the period of a week and you can regulate your thermometer.

Wind Sock

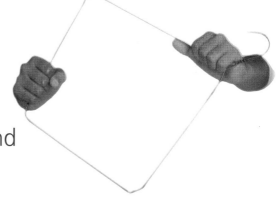

#1   Using a lightweight wire hanger or lightweight wire that is easy to bend, bend the wire into a square.

#2   Cut a square from the trash bag, Visquine, or other plastic material so that one section is the same size as the wire square. Make sure the plastic is light enough to detect slight breezes but strong enough to stand up to gusts of wind.

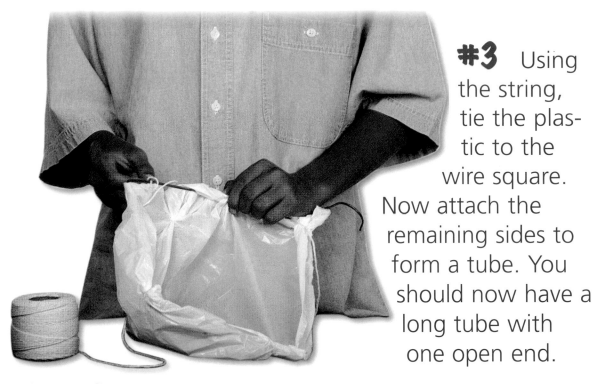

#3 Using the string, tie the plastic to the wire square. Now attach the remaining sides to form a tube. You should now have a long tube with one open end.

Rain Gauge

The rain gauge is the easiest to make of all of the instruments.

#1 With a waterproof marker, mark the clear plastic cup or other container with lines 1 millimeter apart from the bottom to the top. This will allow you to measure the amount of precipitation.

Now you are ready to go on to the next experiment and use your instruments.

2 I'm a Weather Forecaster!

Now that you have constructed your own weather instruments, it is time to use them. This experiment works best when the seasons are changing, but you can try it at any time. Taking each of the items listed, follow the procedures and record your data using copies of the charts on page 17 or your own weather journal. You will soon begin to see patterns in the data and be able to predict what the weather will be for the next day.

Experiment #2

What You Need

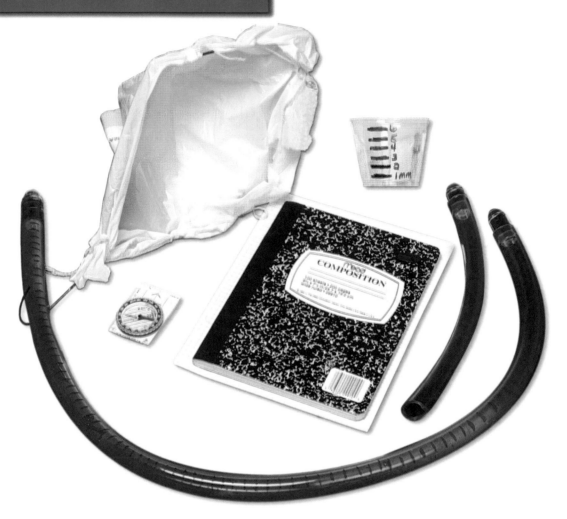

- Your barometer
- Your thermometer
- Your wind sock
- Your rain gauge
- A notebook to use as a weather journal
- Graph paper

Weather Forecaster

What You'll Do

Safety Note: Never go outside during a thunderstorm or lightning storm. Always wear protective clothing and eyewear.

#1 Hang the barometer in a shaded area away from birds and other animals. Make sure you can clearly read the markings.

#2 Hang the thermometer near the barometer. Again, make sure that the area is shaded.

#3 Hang the wind sock in an area where it can move freely in the wind.

#4 Determine which direction is north (use a compass or ask an adult for help), and mark it using a label or stick. Then mark south, west, east, southwest, southeast, northeast, and northwest with a label or stick.

#5 Place the rain gauge out-

doors in a spot where it can easily collect rain as it falls directly to the ground. You do not want to collect runoff from a roof or drainpipe.

#6 Photocopy the graphs on page 17 or make your own on the graph paper. Put the graphs in your note-book. Record all of the measurements from the devices at two times during the day: 7:00 AM and 7:00 PM.

#7 Empty any rainwater that has accumulated each time you check the rain gauge.

#8 Record the actual mea-surements for each day. You can get these from the local weather bureau, the Internet, or the local newspaper. This will give you a good idea of the

Weather Forecaster

accuracy of your measurements. Remember that even if your measurements are not exactly what the newspapers note, they are no less valuable. Your measurements give you a good picture of what is going on in your immediate area. Take these measurements twice a day for one month.

Morning Chart

	Date	Your Measurement	Actual Measurement
Barometer			
Temperature			
Wind			
Rain Amount			

Evening Chart

	Date	Your Meaurement	Actual Measurement
Barometer			
Temperature			
Wind			
Rain Amount			

Experiment #2

Analyzing Your Results

After you have taken measurements for fifteen days, you can begin to forecast. Try to determine what you think will happen the rest of the day, and predict what you think the weather will be the next day. Here are some questions to consider that will help you in predicting the weather. Record your answers in your notebook or weather journal.

#1 Is there any relationship between the barometer reading and the weather?

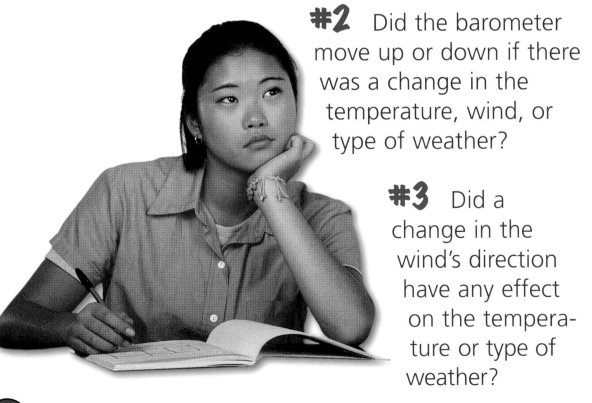

#2 Did the barometer move up or down if there was a change in the temperature, wind, or type of weather?

#3 Did a change in the wind's direction have any effect on the temperature or type of weather?

Weather Forecaster

#4 Did you see any relationship between the measurements from each of the weather instruments and the measurements from the other instruments? How does this relationship relate to the type of weather and to changes in the weather?

#5 How successful were you in forecasting the weather? Were there certain types of weather that were harder to predict than others? What might help you predict the weather more accurately?

For Further Investigation

Using the Internet, track the weather in Asia for two months. Compare the conditions to those in the United States and Canada. Do you see any trends or any cause and effect relationships between Asia's weather and ours? Does severe weather in Asia occur at the same time as particular types of weather in North America?

Have a contest at school to see who can predict the most accurate weather.

If you go on vacation, try predicting the weather while you're there. How does it compare to the weather where you live?

What You Need

- A television, radio, newspaper, or access to a Web site containing forecasts
- A journal or notebook for recording data

What You'll Do

#1 Pick a weather forecaster to follow.

#2 Write down the name of the forecaster and the name of the television or radio station, newspaper, or Web site, and note the date in your journal or notebook.

#3 Record the prediction of high and low temperatures and general weather conditions for the next day. On the following day, record the actual high and low temperatures along with the weather conditions for the previous day. Subtract the actual temperatures from the ones predicted and record the values in your journal.

#4 Record the next day's weather prediction, then record the day's actual values the next day. Continue to record the predicted and actual temperatures, the differences between the two, and the weather conditions for each day until you have a month's worth of data. Weather doesn't stop for weekends, so your notes shouldn't either.

Analyzing Your Results

#1   Graph the differences between the predicted and actual low temperatures. You can photocopy the graph below or make one of your own. Put each day's date on the *x* axis and numbers from 1 to 50 on the *y* axis. Repeat the process on a new graph for the high temperatures.

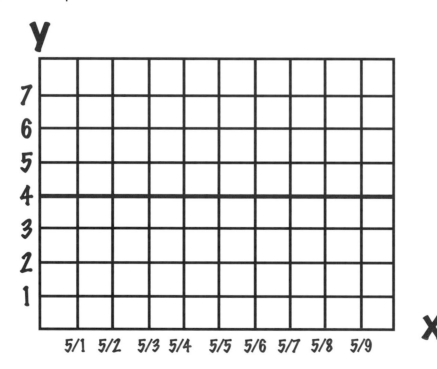

#2   Count how many times the weather forecaster's temperature predictions were correct. Divide that number by the total number of predictions you recorded. The result is the percentage of correct weather forecasts. Record this information in your journal.

#3 Using this same method, calculate the percentage of correct predictions of just the high temperatures, then the percentage for just the low temperatures. In your own estimation, how accurate was your forecaster?

#4 What could your forecaster do to improve his or her accuracy?

For Further Investigation

#1 Repeat the experiment using forecasts from different television or radio stations, newspapers, or Web sites.  Contact a local news program and ask if you can take a tour of the studio and meet the weather forecaster. Find out what he or she does to prepare for a weather report.

#2 Find out how to prepare for a career as a meteorologist. What type of education is required? What types of jobs are available for meteorologists? What salary can a meteorologist expect to earn?

4 Red Sky

Sailors and fishermen have long used a saying to help them decide whether or not they should go to sea: "Red sky at morning, sailors take warning. Red sky at night, sailors delight." This experiment will determine the accuracy of this saying.

According to the saying, the color of the sky in the morning and evening will give sailors an indication of whether the sea will be calm enough to take boats out onto the sea or whether they should stay in the harbor for safety. If the sea is relatively calm, fishing is generally easier, and there is less chance of capsizing.

Fishing was one of the most important industries when our nation first began, and it is still important in some parts of the country. Whether you live by the sea or not, it is very interesting to observe the sky as you watch the weather.

What You Need

- Crayons or colored pencils
- A daily newspaper or access to a nightly television news program
- A notebook to keep notes
- An alarm clock

What You'll Do

#1 Make a color chart like the one below. Using crayons or colored pencils, fill in the chart beginning with red and moving toward violet. You will use this chart to indicate the color of the sky, so it is important to make sure that your colors are distinct. There is an extra section for pink that you would not normally find in a color chart, but you will need this color because it is often found in sunrises and sunsets. Label each color with the first letter of its name. Make at least thirty photocopies or handwritten copies of each of the following charts and put them in your journal or notebook.

Color Chart #1

Red (R)	Pink (P)	Orange (O)	Yellow (Y)	Green (G)	Blue (B)	Violet (V)

#2 Check the times for sunrise and sunset the next day. You can find this information in the newspaper's weather section or on a television weather forecast. Record this information in data chart 1.

Data Chart #1

Time before and after sunrise	Sky color (letter)	Time before and after sunset	Sky color (letter)
-60		-60	
-45		-45	
-30		-30	
-15		-15	
Sunrise		Sunset	
+15		+15	
+30		+30	
+45		+45	
+60		+60	

#3 Now for the hard part! Every morning and evening you must record the color of the sky at 15-minute intervals: one hour before and after sunrise, and one hour before and after sunset.

You will have to go outside to get this data unless you have a clear view of the sunrise and sunset from your window. Be sure to look only at the sky itself. Never look directly at the sun. Try to match the color of the sky to a color on your color chart as closely as possible and record the letter of this color in your chart. It is very important to be as consistent as possible in how you label the colors. If the sky is overcast, record the letters OC.

#4 Now record a description of the day's weather in data chart 2. To simplify things, look at the overall weather for the day. Use descriptions such as stormy, cloudy, sunny, and so forth. Be general in your

Red Sky

Data Chart #2

Date	Weather	Description

description. If you're having trouble describing the weather, look at the descriptions in a weather report on the radio, television, or Internet.

#5 Record your data for a minimum of one month. Remember that part of being a scientist is to keep careful records of the data that will support your conclusions.

Experiment #4

Analyzing Your Results

To help you draw some conclusions about your data, consider the following questions:

#1 Is there any relationship between the weather of the day and the color of the sky in the morning? Is there a relationship between the two in the evening?

#2 Do sailors need to be concerned with the color of the sky? Why or why not?

For Further Investigation

#1 If you have access to the Internet, try searching for Web sites that have television cameras with live displays of different places. Television stations in many large cities, including Los Angeles, New York, Chicago, and Memphis, have cameras that record the sights and sounds of the day at a particular spot. Bookmark these sites, then visit them each day and record the color of the sky in your chart. Check the daily weather forecasts and reports of current conditions; this will give you excellent data on which to base your conclusions.

Red Sky

Follow the same instructions you used for recording the weather conditions outside, and record your data.

#2 Search the Web to find some sites that have weather information. This is a large task, but you will be rewarded with

interesting facts and information on weather.

5 Sky View

Part of being a good meteorologist is being alert to the current weather conditions. By being aware of what is happening now, a meteorologist can determine what the weather will be in the future.

Before you start, make sure to study the glossary at the end of this book so that you can describe the clouds and sky accurately. Scientists like to know what other scientists see, so they use a vocabulary that they have agreed on.

What You Need

- A journal or notebook
- A pencil or pen for taking notes

What You'll Do

#1 Decide on three to five times during the day to observe the sky. Choose times that are at least a few hours apart to get a good idea of the conditions throughout the day.

#2   Record the time and date and a description of the sky using the numbers from the following weather guide. Using these numbers makes it easier to record the conditions and makes the data collection more consistent. You may wish to add some more descriptions to your guide, depending on the weather in your area.

#3 Never, never go out to make observations when lightning or severe weather conditions exist. The people who chase storms are trained, experienced professionals. No one else should try to observe a storm close up.

You will have at least two indicators: wind and clouds.

Weather Guide

Wind:

None **1**   Breezy **2**   Windy **3**   High Wind **4**

Clouds:

Sunny **5**   Partly Cloudy **6**   Overcast **7**   Dark Clouds **8**

Sample Data Chart

Date	Time	Conditions

Analyzing Your Results

Make a data chart like the one on this page in your journal, and record your observations.

#1 Have you discovered a relationship between the wind and the resulting overall weather conditions?

#2 Do you see any patterns in the day-to-day conditions?

#3 What relationship exists among the conditions recorded at different times throughout the day?

6 Looking at Lightning

Lightning is a gigantic burst of electrical activity in the clouds or between clouds and the ground. The energy released in a lightning strike is power-ful—and dangerous. Lightning is one of the most

violent acts of nature. If you have ever been in a thunderstorm and witnessed a sudden, explosive bolt of lightning, you know the power of this weather phe-nomenon. In this experiment, you will learn about lightning without putting yourself in danger. Never go outside to observe a thunderstorm in which there are multiple lightning strikes. Lightning is nothing to take lightly.

Everything in the universe is made up of incredibly tiny particles called atoms. Atoms can carry a positive, negative, or neutral electrical charge. When negatively and positively charged particles move toward each other, they cause a spark. When this occurs inside a cloud or between a cloud and an object on the ground, the spark that forms is what we know as lightning. No one is exactly sure how clouds become electrically charged, but we do know that this occurs all the time.

This is a research activity, but before you start yawning, give it a try! You'll learn something that will put you in awe of how a small part of nature works. Without lightning, you wouldn't be here. Find out why.

What You Need

- A journal or notebook
- A pencil
- Access to a library or the Internet

What You'll Do

#1 Using your research sources, make the following observations and answer the following questions. In your journal, draw the lightning bolt from the initial formation to the time of discharge.

Looking at Lightning

#2 Count the lightning strikes in a storm and record the number in your journal. Do this for several different storms. Research the number of lightning strikes in an average storm. How do the storms in your area compare to the average?

#3 Which way does the bolt of lightning appear to go, from the ground to the clouds or the clouds to the ground? Does the flash of light really travel this way? Why or why not?

#4 A coulomb is a measure of the electrical attraction between two particles. How many coulombs are in a typical lightning strike?

#5 Where in the United States does lightning strike most often? Why? Where in the world does it strike most often? Why?

#6 What are the favorable conditions for lightning to strike?

#7 How can you create a small-scale lightning strike in your home? Hint: It's easiest in winter after you've walked across the carpet.

#8 Why is lightning important?

#9 Why is it dangerous?

Looking at Lightning

For Further Investigation

Consider the following and write your responses in your journal.

#1 What do you think would happen to our world if there was never another lightning strike?

#2 How can human beings protect themselves and their property from lightning?

#3 What was Benjamin Franklin's importance in the study of lightning? What does a lightning rod do?

#4 What would happen if the number of lightning strikes increased?

#5 What precautions should we take to avoid being struck by lightning?

glossary

air pressure   The weight of the air in the atmosphere on one particular spot at one specific moment.

atom   The tiny particles of which everything on earth is made.

barometer   A device that measures air pressure.

coulomb   A measurement of the electrical attraction between two atoms or particles.

humidity   The amount of moisture in the air.

meteorologist   A scientist who studies weather and the atmosphere.

weather forecaster   Someone (usually a meteorologist) who analyzes the current weather, typical weather at particular times of year, and other weather data and tries to predict what the next day's or week's weather will be.

resources

These Web sites will help you learn more about weather.

Cloud Catalog—Guide to Meteorology
http://couis.atmos.uiuc.edu/guide/clouds/html/oldhome.html

Cool Science for Curious Kids
http://www.hhmi.org/coolscience

Cyberspace Middle School—Science Fair Projects
http://www.scri.fsu.edu/~dennisl/special/sf_projects.html

Earth Studies
http://www.indirect.com/www/dhixson/earth.html

The Environmental Protection Agency's Global Warming Web Site
http://www.epa.gov/globalwarming/home.htm

Environment Canada's Green Lane
http://www.ec.gc.ca

Exploratorium
http://www.exploratorium.edu

Explore the World—Owl Kids Online
http://www.owl.on.ca

The Internet Schoolhouse
http://www.onr.com/schoolhouse/

Mad Scientist Network
http://www.madsci.org

Newton Ask a Scientist
http://newton.dep.anl.gov/aasquest.htm

The Science Club
http://www.halcyon.com.sciclub/kidquest.html

Science Fair Project Ideas
http://othello.mech.nwu.edu/~peshkin/scifair/index.html

Scientific American Explore!
http://www.sciam.com/explorations

The Weather Channel
http://www.weather.com

for further reading

Deacon, Andrew. *Weatherworks: The Book and Workshop.* Philadelphia, PA: Running Press, 1998.

Elsom, Derek. *Weather Explained: A Beginner's Guide to the Elements.* New York: Henry Holt & Co., 1997.

Galliano, Dean. *Clouds, Rain, and Snow.* New York: Rosen Publishing Group, 1999.

———. *Thunderstorms and Lightning.* New York: Rosen Publishing Group, 1999.

Kahl, Jonathan. *Weather Watch: Forecasting the Weather.* Minneapolis, MN: Lerner Publications, 1996.

Lampton, Christopher F. *Drought: A Disaster Book.* New York: Houghton Mifflin Co., 1992.

———. *Hurricane: A Disaster Book.* New York: Houghton Mifflin, 1992.

Ramsey, Dan. *Weather Forecasting: A Young Meteorologist's Guide.* New York: McGraw-Hill Professional Book Group, 1990.

Silverstein, Alvin. *Weather and Climate.* New York: Twenty-First Century Books, 1998.

Taylor-Cork, Barbara. *Weather Forecaster.* Danbury, CT: Franklin Watts, 1992.

Wagner, Ronald L., and Bill Adler Jr. *The Weather Sourcebook.* Old Saybrook, CT: Globe Pequot Press, 1994.

index

Credits

Acknowledgments
Thanks to Amy Smallwood, Peggy Whittaker, and Faye Werner, who helped me put the book in human form.

About the Author
Lorraine Jones is a middle school science teacher in Tennessee.

Photo Credits
Cover photos by Scott Bauer. Pp. 4, 20, 21 & 41 © Warren Faidley/International Stock; p. 6 © CORBIS/Roger Ressmeyer; pp. 25 & 33 by Thaddeus Harden; p. 26 © CORBIS/Craig Aurness; p. 34 © CORBIS/Tim Wright. All other photographs by Scott Bauer.

Design and Layout
Laura Murawski

Consulting Editors
Annie Sommers and Amy Haugesag

Metric Conversions
To convert measurements in U.S. units into metric units, use the following formulas:

1 inch = 2.54 centimeters (cm)	1 ounce = 28.35 grams (g)
1 foot = 0.30 meters (m)	1 gallon = 3.79 liters (l)
1 mile = 1.609 kilometers (km)	1 pound = 453.59 grams (g)